WHISPERS
IN MY SOUL

Yvonne "Cooky" Tavares

xulon PRESS

10-19-16

DEAR CAROLYN, EVERY
"I THANK GOD UPON EVERY
REMEMBRANCE OF YOU." I
AT MY VERY 1st AGLOW RETREAT
SOME TWENTY YEARS AGO AT KALIHI VALLEY,
OAHU IS WHERE I 1st MET YOU.
NANCY the DANIEL WAS DOING THE WORSHIP
AND PLAYING KEYBOARD. IT WAS A BEAUTIFUL
THE CHAPEL OF WORSHIP. WHEN YOU ENTERED
ATMOSPHERE OF PURE LOVE WAS RELEASED
THE LOVE OVERFLOWING AND BUBBLING OUT LIKE
A RIVER OF JESUS IN YOU. POURING OVER.
THAT SAME LOVE OF JESUS IS A BEAUTIFUL
MANTLE WITHIN AND OVER YOUR LIFE.
I LOVE YOU UNTO
FOREVER. COOKY

THANK-YOU OH MIGHTY WOMEN
OF GOD & YOUR LOVE SETTING CAPTIVES
FREE!

Endorsements

There are many people that touch our lives in our journey through this earth, but few that touch our souls. Cooky Tavares is one that has not only touched my soul, but has reached deep, spirit to spirit. This is the divine relationship she has with her Heavenly Father. She is His daughter, friend, mouth piece, and warrior bride. The call of intimacy with her Papa God has always been of a deep unto deep experiential cry. Song of Solomon 2:8 and 5:2 says, "I sleep but my heart waketh: it is the voice of my Beloved that knocketh. Behold, He cometh leaping upon the mountains skipping upon the hills…" Such is Cooky's love song for her Father God. There is a yearning to touch the Heart of God and the desire to only do His will. To kindle a fire so bright in her inner most being, she then releases that desire into those lives the Lord entrusts her with. She is an Aglow Woman. She is Aglow and burning in the Spirit. My prayer is that an awakening spirit be released as you read the pages of Cooky's story "Whispers in my Soul". This is Life in the Spirit.

"For I do always those things that please Him" John 8:29

Pastor Lani Bair

The Village Church Volcano Assembly of God

Hawaii State Prayer Coordinator, Aglow International

Whispers in My Soul is a must read for anyone who thinks they have no future with God.

The author openly shares her life to reach out and encourage others to give them hope in their journey. Her heart of love for all people and all of the Church are evident as she shares her story. We need to know the healing power of God in our lives and trust Him as the Author does to lead us to a life full of joy and peace in Him. I know this book will touch your life in a positive way.

Carolyn Suty

Aglow International

Southwest Regional Director

Life is a journey! In our journey is destiny! It was more than 20 years ago that destiny brought Cooky and I together on the Big Island of Hawaii. I was speaking at a women's conference and the the night before I had a dream that I was ministering to a teenage girl. On the morning of the conference, I could not believe my eyes when Cooky came walking in with her teenage daughter, Tyson. She was the girl in my dream. Destiny!

Throughout these 20 odd years, our journey has brought us together year-after-year. We have grown together in the Lord and labored together with God to advance His Kingdom on Earth. If there was one phrase that would describe this mighty woman of God it would be, "God's Gifted Encourager." But I would add to this that she is a carrier of God's love, a mighty warrior, a prophetess whom God has set a trumpet to her mouth to be a voice to this generation in sounding the alarm. She is an amazing communicator, a woman of God whom I greatly admire and love.

As you walk with Cooky on her journey in "Whispers In My Soul," you will encounter her real-life experiences and enjoy her deep and personal relationship with her "Papa God" as He whispers in her soul the secrets of life and calls her to "come up higher."

I highly endorse and recommend "Whispers In My Soul" as a source of personal direction and spiritual growth for your life's journey. From beginning to end you will be captivated by her personal stories and life lessons. Wherever you are in your journey, this book will offer hope to meet the challenges and changes in your life. Let it be a launching pad into your destiny and, perhaps, only a whisper away from your encounter with "Papa God," who may be calling you to "come up higher."

Semmie Hollifield

The Barnabas Walk

Table Of Contents

CHAPTER ONE

Deep Calls Unto Deep

There's a deep wooing in my Spirit. I hear the voice of the One I love calling unto me: "Come up higher, come up higher my beloved. Come and dine with me. I will show you what eyes have not seen, and what ears have not heard."

"Here I am," I reply, "Please speak to me, oh Lord; your daughter is listening." The presence of the one majestic God overshadows me and I am swept into perfect peace, rest, joy, and love. I can hardly contain myself with such delight. I am deeply humbled my King has called me. I am astonished, overcome, and overwhelmed by His great love and kindness toward me.

I hear the gentle whisper of my Lord speak to me, as He says, "My beloved one, hold fast on the promises that are yours, for they will come to pass. Stay under the shelter of my wings and prosper in all you do. For you have been chosen and your calling is a threat to the enemy's camp. Stay on guard! For even now, I am sending reinforcement. You are surrounded by heavenly armies. Yes, you are a warrior in my Kingdom, and the flag that is raised, is triumph!" My story is one of overcoming. In 1954, as a toddler I was admitted to Kona Hospital in critical condition. The doctors could not help me as my life continued to decline. I was unable to maintain nourishment due to relentless vomiting. In Hawaii, it is known as Huli Opu or twisted stomach/intestines in English. There have been numerous tragic deaths from this ailment if it is not intervened upon early. Keep in mind, in those days, medical interventions were quite limited. At that time in history, Kona had only a few practicing licensed physicians, and they did it all. The medical staff did not allow anyone to enter my room because of the acuteness of my condition. However, my parents and family relentlessly sought help outside the practice of mainstream medicine. A Portuguese woman who was known in the community for praying over infants and healing by way of stomach massage was snuck into my hospital room. She prayed the breaking of curses and did a Holy Spirit therapeutic massage intervention and treatment. She not only treated the physical ailments, but also the spiritual.

Through that key intervention, I was miraculously healed. That day would be the first of many times that the enemy tried to take me out. I thank God that He intervened early in my life. We have guardian angels assigned to us. God sustains us for the fulfillment of the plans and purposes for our lives from generation to generation. God saved Moses as a babe from Pharaoh's death decree upon the Hebrew boys born at that time. He would later lead a nation into freedom. God saved me from the clutches of death also so the plans and purposes He has for my life can likewise be fulfilled.

In retrospect, as I ponder that phase of my early beginnings and what would follow, I realize the gravity of prayer covering and divine intervention. The power of life in the spirit is allocated to us for our overcoming victory. The battle is real.

This story of mine would have absolutely no meaning without proclaiming Jesus as Lord and savior in my life. My prayer is you would see Jesus through my story. For He alone is the way, the truth, and the life. There is no life or story without Him. He turns ashes into beauty. He makes the impossible possible. He alone makes all things new.

This Book is dedicated to the Holy Triune, the one and only God. To Father God whose love endures forever and whose mercies and grace are new everyday. To Jesus, my Lord and Savior, who took my sins upon the cross and set me free from darkness. To the Holy Spirit, who lives within me, gently guiding, teaching, loving, and empowering me each day to look more and more like Jesus.

Unless my fragrance becomes a complete fragrance of Heaven in Him, I will not be satisfied. There is a hunger and a thirst for more. There is a call to arise and come up higher. Will we listen to the call, will we go, will we walk in obedience?

Like Mary, the Mother of our King Jesus, let this, oh Lord, be my fiat as well: "Be it done to me Lord, according to your will." It is my "yes" declared, oh Lord! My soul doth magnify the Lord in the image and presence of Christ within me.

CHAPTER TWO

Where's My Kingdom

Whispers in my soul, as I hear my Father speak, "I love you! Be still; be anxious for nothing. For I have a plan for all things. I cover the plans and purposes I have for your life. You are covered, my beloved, with robes of holiness and righteousness. You are covered with the majesty of my presence. My glory shall be seen throughout the nations. There is no darkness in my light. You, beloved sons and daughters, are children of the light. Shine beloved, shine. For the glory of your creator is upon you. I share my light with no other, but you, beloved, are mine. You are mine! Rest now in the shadow of the Almighty. Your journey has only just begun."

"He who dwells in the secret place of the most high shall abide under the shadow of the almighty."

–Psalm 91:1-2

I was born and raised in Kona, Hawaii on the Big Island. My mother, Erna, was a German Fraulein who captured my father Graciano's heart during his US military service in Germany following World War II. In 1953, my mom (then pregnant with me, the third of five children) and dad moved back to the island of Hawaii where my father was born. He was the first generation of Rivera born in Hawaii after my grandfather migrated from Puerto Rico. I had a colorful, playful, happy, and disciplined childhood. Good times were balanced with summers harvesting coffee on my parents' five-acre coffee farm. During my childhood, teen years, and beyond, my parents' incredible work ethic impacted my life. Learning hard work, responsibility, honesty, love, and valuable life lessons fashioned my life and my journey.

I embraced the different cultures and never understood segregation, prejudices, and hate for people of different color or culture. My extended family was a blend of many races including German, Puerto Rican, Hawaiian, Portuguese, Chinese, English, and more.

As the generations grew, the intermarriages expanded with the inclusion of even more cultures that are now *ohana* (family). As the years went by, I came to realize the subtleties of prejudice that was also apart of the culture in which I was raised. Though people groups learned to co-exist, there were still labeling and unkind voices and messages released.

With the passing of years, I felt a deep sense of, "Where then do I belong?" I am not by blood a Kanaka Maoli (one whose lineage can be traced back to the first Polynesians in the Kingdom of Hawaii), but this is where I was born on this land and this is my home.

After fifty plus years of life on the islands, roots become deeply planted. As so was the case with my mother. I now pray blessing over that young Polynesian man, no more than thirty years old, who cursed my mom in the parking lot on the way to breakfast. Mom traveled over a hundred miles from the west side of the island to visit with me. We planned to meet for breakfast. While walking from the parking lot to the restaurant, curses were hurled at her, "Go back to where you came from, *haole*!" As I pointed out, she had been in the islands over fifty years and loved Hawaii and her extended *ohana* of Hawaiian lineage. However, that day, her heart was so sad for the hate that was spewed at her for the color of her skin. There was a deep sadness upon her as we met for breakfast. Had I witnessed what happened, I would have been tempted to give him a sweet Hawaiian punch. Yet, God spared the drama that day. My mom was a woman of a different spirit. The banner over her was love.

So then, where's my kingdom, Lord? Is it in Germany? Is it in Puerto Rico? Oh wait, did you somehow connect your kingdom to mine and it now lives in Hawaii? What kingdom am I in? Lights on—revelation time. I am not of this world and this is not my kingdom.

> "If you belonged to the world, then the world would love you as its own. But I chose you from the world, and you do not belong to it; that is why the world hates you." –John 15:19

Whose voice did I listen to anyway? Now that I know what kingdom I'm from, and the Kingdom of God is within me, how's that going for me and you and what does that lifestyle look like? Are our feet planted in the right kingdom?

Whispers in my soul, as I hear my Father speak, "Stay the course, stand for holiness, and righteousness. Stand for all that I pour down upon you. All that I am, stand! For you were created to stand in holiness, stand in righteousness, stand in mercy, stand in goodness, stand in kindness, stand in compassion, stand in courage, stand in wisdom, stand in knowledge, stand in love, and in the holy fear of the Lord."

"Be alert, stand firm in the faith, be brave, be strong.
Do all your work in love." – 1 Corinthians 16:13-14

There was a time when that concept felt foreign to me. Like Mercury and Mars, giants and giant slayers, free or not. There were too many voices in the kingdom of the world and none of them led me to the one true kingdom.

A life of debauchery would be my path. Choosing the road of hard knocks and living with the consequences of this death culture left me empty, depressed, oppressed, fearful, faithless, hopeless, worthless, ugly, and wanting to sign out of here. Yes, that was me. I failed two suicide attempts and entertained the thought of just dieing numerous times..Yes, the battlefield was in my mind! Oh, but for the prayers of those who interceded in my behalf from even before I was in my mother's womb. Oh, but for the mercy, grace, divine intervention, and love of God for me, where would I be?

Now you must be wondering, *I thought she said she had a happy childhood?* Well yes, I did, but those tumultuous teenage years of rebellion, free religion, free sex, and free everything became me. I became that which I knew was not in God's plan for me. I did it my way and didn't once think what doors I would spiritually give satan's camp authority to enter. It was like the cloud of God's presence in Egypt lifted and a cloud of darkness loomed. That dark day turned into months before miraculous healing would follow as God's mercy and good intentions for my life would win that battle over the Kingdom of Darkness.

Whispers in my soul, I hear the Father speak future destiny. "You are called as Prophet and Prophetess, a voice crying out in the desert. Make your ways straight. Repent while there is still time. Darkness covers the earth and so many have been caught in satan's web of lies, evil, lust, and sin. The world calls good, "evil," and evil, "good." My daughter, I have called you to be my voice in those parched places. You have bravely and courageously spoken the truth. You have faced rejection, gossip, persecution, and unbelief.

You continue to press on as a defender of faith. I shelter you, my beloved. Be lifted high upon the rock of your salvation. For I have chosen you to be a voice proclaiming and declaring my Word. Be not discouraged beloved, for I am with you always."

The Lord comes to me in an open vision. I see the eye of God and within moments, it changes into the Lion of Judah. I am left with immeasurable peace as the comfort of our Father's eye is upon the Lion and me and the Lamb, King Jesus, conveys His kingship throughout all tribulation and persecution. The Lion who rules the nations and the Lamb who takes away the sins of the world reigns supreme. There is hope for the lost.

> "Repent therefore and be converted that your sins
> may be blotted out, so that times of refreshing may
> come from the Presence of the Lord." –Acts 3:19

Though the doors of hell were open, the Lord looked upon me with great mercy, forgiveness, and love.

What doors and how is that possible?

CHAPTER THREE

Doos Of Evil Or Good

Nehemiah wept and fasted for the people of Israel. Before he received a vision from the Lord, he knew the power of intercession, repentance, and fasting. When foundations are broken, evil enters. I too cried out with a broken and repentive heart. It starts with the cleansing of your own soul so you can mature in your walk and begin to take cities, territories, and nations. I declare all the breached and broken walls will be mended. I proclaim that as we stand on the Word of God, spiritual hedges will be an unbreakable wall of the Kingdom of God united in unity and love as one.

In Matthew 15:19-20, God's Word says, "out of our heart proceeds evil thoughts, murders, adulteries, fornications, thefts, false witness, and blasphemies." These are the things that defile us, otherwise known as sin. When we yield to those things, we are giving the enemy's camp an entrance to have access to our soul, which is the seat of our mind, will, and emotions.

By being rebellious, I opened the door to hear the whispers of the enemy of my soul justify the poor choices and wrong path that I chose. Whispers told me it's acceptable to engage in relationships outside of covenantal marriage. Everybody else does. Have fun. Have another drink. How about some weed? Try something new like cocaine, speed, or LSD. It's okay. Soon it will be legalized anyway. Through all of that mire, daily prayer, going to church, or reading my Bible became something I did in my childhood and in my youth. Now I am an adult and can do what I want to do. It's all about me—or is it? Now I am in deep bondage. Heaven wept while hell applauded my demise.

But God! I am sorry; I know this is wrong. If it is so right, why do I feel so empty, so alone, so guilty, so ashamed, and so lost with no hope for a future or a plan? Not even a small vision or a goal, but more debauchery leading to nowhere. Surely, oh Lord, you forgave King David and he was an adulterer and a murderer. Surely God, you forgave Mary Magdalene, the prostitute. Surely God, you forgave Saul, the persecutor of Christians. Is there any hope for me? Will you break these chains that bind and keep me captive? Is there forgiveness left for me? Will you give me back my key? Jesus you are the KEY! You've taken my sin and those of the whole world upon the cross so that we would be set free. You who were without sin took our transgressions.

"You, oh Lord who had no sin became sin" (2 Corinthians 5:21). You were the offering of my sin so I might become the righteousness of God. Repentance is a powerful weapon. What happened next was how God broke those chains.

CHAPTER FOUR

Break Every Chain

Whispers in my soul, I hear my Father speaking to me, "Be not afraid of what is coming. Great shaking and greater awakening. It is my plan from the beginning that not one would be lost. All branches that are not fruitful must be cut down and burnt. I have come for a spotless bride. A bride consumed by my fire. It is time to sound the Shofar. It is time!"

> The word of God is alive and active, sharper than any double-edged sword. It cuts all the way through, to where soul and spirit meet, to where joints and marrow come together. It judges the desires and thoughts of the heart. There is nothing that can be hid from God; everything in all creation is

exposed and lies open before his eyes. And it is to him that we must all give an account of ourselves. Hebrews 4:12-13

Sometimes we have to hit rock bottom before we can get up. That's the place that in desperation, my heart cried out to the Lord. I could no longer function. Delusional thoughts, obsessed behavior, and fear ruled my life. I tried my best to maintain a semblance of sanity by showing up for work at the Naniloa Loa Surf Hotel as a front office clerk. On my time off, I would jog five miles a day, watched every calorie that I consumed, and lost so much weight that I looked drawn and undernourished. My social time was spent smoking weed, partying, and cultivating marijuana crops with my boyfriend. Surely we thought we would get rich by selling dope.

Whenever I picked up a book to read, it was never an edifying read. The Bible was something I picked up when I wanted to pluck the log out of somebody else's eye for being so evil. At the time, there appeared to be a few others who appeared to need a lot more deliverance than I did. Warning: if that's you, back up. That got me in a whole lot of spiritual trouble to add to the list of demons that already had a party in my life. The moment I did that, with my own dirty rags as a mantle, and I started preaching deliverance for someone else in need, that spirit got delivered, but then came to party with my demons. That was the day deep darkness camped around me. My boyfriend could no longer cope with my craziness and called my parents to come get me. He couldn't handle it. I accused him of being unfaithful. I kept night watches with a gun, a Bible, and a sword, thinking I had to be vigilant and on guard for the evil that tried to enter our apartment. In my delusional mind, I protected the love of my life, my boyfriend. Evil entered all right, but it was in my abode.

Well, my parents did come. Needless to say, they were in utter shock at how I had regressed to a place of not being lucid in my thinking. They immediately called 911 and admitted me to the county hospital. I was so out there, they had to refer me to the head of psychiatry. I was admitted to the psychiatric unit. That was forty years ago and the memory of the horror and drama remains.

What psychiatry doesn't heal, God will; God uses the impossible to show himself faithful. So many prayed for me. Then God did the unexpected. He sent a Catholic Priest, Father Joseph Avery, to deliver me from this darkness. Keep in mind: I was a baptized born-again, back-sliding Protestant. As a child and youth, I attended the first Christian church on the island. I went to Sunday school, Vacation Bible School, and religious education. I belonged to the church *keiki* (little children) and youth choir. I always had a heart that loved the Lord and wanted to see my entire family saved.

Yet, God never left me; I shut Him out and allowed the whispers of doubt, fear, and faithlessness to enter. They trumped over the sound of heaven in my life. Sin, unrepentance, rebellion, pride, and lustfulness ruled my life. After one week in the mental ward, I had had enough! The craziness of that environment was not an open heaven experience. The moment the nurse was out of visual proximity, I put on my fuzzy pink booties and bolted out the door with the speed of a gazelle. For sure, bolted exit doors were implemented thereafter.

Within ten minutes, I was a mile away from the hospital, running my way back home to my apartment. By then, my boyfriend and parents were informed and they were beside themselves in worry about my safety. However, executive hotel boss to the rescue: she saw me in sprint mode and offered to drive me home. That was a good thing, because that would convince her of how crazy I was since I would be out on sick leave for a while. Well, that great escape led to God's plan for my deliverance.

My boyfriend and parents drove me to the church that Father Avery pastored. It was twenty miles away in the Puna District of Hawaii. That day, a miracle took place. With the rosary in his hand (another weapon of mass destruction to Catholics), he made me follow along with every prayer. That was a first for me. I then wept and went into automatic repentive mode. It was in the spirit of a contrite and broken heart. I conveyed how I hated my sinful life and repented of every dark and evil way of life that I rebelliously lived. I cried out to God for forgiveness. The priest counseled me in his great wisdom and took the oil of healing and anointed my forehead. As my sins were absolved, I physically felt a spiritual entity leave me. From the top of my head, like a whoosh, it was gone. Perhaps not as dramatic as an exorcism, but truthfully, rather close. What my parents and boyfriend witnessed after that was a completely changed demeanor and countenance. I was delivered. The affect of that took months of healing as God poured His goodness into former dark places in my soul. I continued therapy, both in the natural and the spiritual.

Within a year, I was diagnosed again and was told I was misdiagnosed and didn't have the classical symptoms that would indicate otherwise. Still, God knows it was so much more than a DSM diagnosis of schizophrenia. It was legal rights I freely gave to the kingdom of darkness when I chose to lead a life of debauchery.

Ever wonder why so many patients fill the wards of mental hospitals and many more wander the streets? Why do some get healed and delivered and others don't? Well, I think about that because after my experience of being set free, I wanted the same for every mental health patient. Some things are still a mystery. Now that my old sinful nature was dead, I learned to embrace my new self. The confident and strong woman that God created me to be came alive. It has, however, taken at least forty years to discover the fullness of the restored new man and abundant life in the spirit. It is in that place that spiritual growth has exponentially taken me to new heights in the spirit realm.

God continues to whisper to me, "Come up higher my beloved, come up higher. There is more." The whispers of gloom, doom and defeat are gone. It is buried and dead. I recognize those negative voices, should they even try to enter. I've overcome those days and nights of darkness by trading in my dirty rags for robes of righteousness and holiness. That was the old me, but it will forever serve as a reminder of the Kingdoms of Good and Evil and in what kingdom I stand secure. When you stand firmly in the right Kingdom, you are under a different atmosphere. There is a different language, a different thinking, and a different outcome in your life. How do you know what kingdom you are in?

CHAPTER FIVE

Kingdom Culture

"Jesus answered, 'My kingdom is not of this world. If my kingdom were of this world, my servants would have fought that I might not be delivered up to the Jews. But now my kingdom is not from here.'" –John 18:36

God's kingdom culture reigns sovereign and supreme over all cultures and all kingdoms. It is His intentional and sovereign plan for mankind. The kingdom of God begins in the heart of redeemed men and women.

"For he has rescued us from the dominion of darkness and brought us into the kingdom of the Son
he loves." –Colossians 1:13

The world's cultures, depending on where you are from, reflects beliefs, values, customs, behaviors, and historical pieces that are passed on from one generation to the next. God created the world and all that is in it. Every nation is a thought, heartbeat, breath, and sound of the treasures of God's creation. We were created to rule and reign in God's Kingdom on earth as it is in heaven.

Twenty years ago, in the city of Hilo, Hawaii, the Lord pulled upon my heartstrings to leadership with what was formerly known as the Women's Aglow. We are now a global ministry, and for the past sixteen years, have walked in an upgraded call as warriors and champions in God's Kingdom. We are no longer Women's Aglow. We have been reestablished and rooted by God as Aglow International and are currently in 170 nations and six continents. The Lord has a beautiful way of whispering in our hearts to be a part of things that will not only expand the Kingdom of God, but also securely help to grow and cultivate that which He has planted. We have been woven into many parts of the body. What brings great delight, glory, and honor to our Father is when we truly walk in unity and love as one. All of heaven rejoices and hell shudders as the kingdom of darkness falls. We are a culture of game-changers and life-changers.

In our 2014 Summit Leadership meeting, one of our advisors, Graham Cooke reminded us of what a game-changer is. A game-changer is someone who's been changed beyond recognition, someone on a new journey with no negative thinking. We are creating a different story. We are seeing things differently. We are arising and occupying new places in anointing. We no longer are giving flesh to the enemy. We are seeing who God is for us. When faced with hell, trials, tribulations, or suffering, we learn to rise above all circumstances. Through this encounter, process, and revelation, our story is changing. We are declaring we are living on a higher place. We are cultivating the fruit of the spirit. We are clothed in His presence and walking in the fullness now. Glory to God! We are kingdom-minded warriors. Our story is changing as we rise from glory to glory on earth as it is in heaven.

Are we all-in? We are as Graham prophetically said, "Being seriously upgraded in the things of the Spirit" and we need to be all-in.

Chuck Pierce said the three generations are aligning like never before. Glory is rising! Are you all-in? What kingdom are you in?

Whispers in my soul, I hear my Father's voice speaking, "Listen, listen my beloved. Do you hear the sound of my presence? Sometimes a quiet whisper. Sometimes a wind afresh upon you. Immerse, my beloved. Immerse yourself in who I am for you. Let your steps be guided by my spirit alone. I go before you to soften the ground you walk on. I place my sound within you. Release a new sound, beloved. Release the sound of love, release the sound of joy. Release the sound of victory. Listen, listen, do you hear the sound? The beautiful whispers of my Father's voice continues in my soul. Listen, again, I say, listen. Have you heard me calling you? I have called you by name. I know everything about you and I love you. I see who you are and I see who you are becoming. Did I not say I would never leave or abandon you? I lift you up when you fall. I raise you up high upon the rock of my mercy. I cover you with my protection and with my love. For you are mine, beloved. You are mine. Stay under my shelter and love."

It's easy to be celebratory and joyful during happy times, but how is that working for us when faced with trials, tribulation, suffering, and bad reports? Will we be blown to and fro, whine, complain, find fault, or someone to blame, condemn, judge, entertain pity parties, or will we press deeper into God through prayer, reading His word, knowing our identity in Christ, and having a faith in His promises that will never waver? What will that cost? What does that look like?

CHAPTER SIX

The Cost

Since, then you have been raised with Christ. Set your heart on things above, where Christ is, seated at the right hand of God. Set your minds on things above not on earthly things. For you died, and your life is now hidden with Christ in God. When Christ, who is in your life, appears, then you will also appear with him in glory. – Colossians 3:1-4

If you continue to choose a life of debauchery, chances are, you will bypass the rest of Colossians because it's quite clear what earthly nature must be put to death. That, beloved, will cost. Are you willing to embrace and live the Kingdom of God culture? It may rattle your world if you are holding tightly to the world's culture of beliefs and what I call the "culture of death" because of how it sucks the life out of you. There is no life without life in the spirit. There is no light where the oil runs out.

Think of Saint Stephen, the first martyr. It cost him his life. He remained faithful and being full of the Holy Spirit, gazed into heaven before he died. His last words were that of forgiveness. He forgave those who stoned him to death. In our own generation, there are numerous others who counted the cost by not renouncing the one true God at the fate of death sentence by Islamic radicals.

To truly follow Christ, we must count the cost and put Him above everything else. It is a higher call. It is where the seed of God's Kingdom is cultivated and grown. The nature of God becomes more and more visible in our lives as we know who we are in Christ. We are made in His image, not the other way around. We are called to holiness, righteousness, morality, honesty, faithfulness, truthfulness, integrity, kindness, goodness, humility, meekness, self-control, and more. It's a life of repentance and overcoming victory. Should we fall, the grace and mercy of God honors our supplication and provides all that we need to get back up and ascend once more. A repentant heart does not give the enemy a foothold if we truly turn and walk in the opposite spirit. Remember that key that I mentioned earlier? Well, if there are evil and good doors, there must be keys to open and shut things. Oh Lord, you've entrusted me with keys.

> "I will give you the keys of the Kingdom of heaven; and whatever you bind on earth shall have been bound in heaven, and whatever you loose on earth shall have been loosed in heaven." – Matthew 16:19

KEYS OF AUTHORITY

Whispers in my soul, I hear my Father say, "Stay the course. Have I not told you that greater works will you do, see and be apart of? It is time to rise up higher and take the mantle of authority and victory to restore the captives and to plunder the enemy's camp. Let your lamp be overflowing with the oil of my spirit. For, yes, you are not alone. There is victory ahead!"

"My mercy runs deep for my children. I am the giver of life. The river of life flows with my abundant streams of mercy and grace. I am your portion and reward. Drink, drink from the fountain of life. Be refreshed for the journey. I am your refreshment and inheritance. Receive great heavenly flow of blessings."

The Whispers speak deeper into my soul and my spirit arises. "Hope is the faith of things unseen. The hope of glory is within you. Unlock the treasures of hope. I've given you the key of hope, it is a pearl of great price. Open up your treasure box."

Declaring, proclaiming and decreeing that this is the season of breakthrough. Beleiving for the healing and restoration over families, cities, churches, and nations. Declaring a shadow like Peter's is arising that is bringing healing to multitudes and setting captives free. It's already here!

What kingdom are you building? Did you misplace your keys?

CHAPTER SEVEN

Building The Kingdom

Will your building pass the code of inspection? Did you study the blueprints given to you by the master builder? Now you should have the perfect plan, strategy, and a vision. Ready to run with it? Before you start building, you will need oil that never runs out. You are going to need lots of fuel for this house. You can't do it with the cheap stuff. Jesus paid with His life so make sure your oil vessels are overflowing.

Have you read the blueprints yet? I mean, from front to back. Like Genesis to Revelation? Well get on it, then. You won't know how to open that big door if you don't know where the keyholes are! Did you ask God about the plan the strategy and the vision? You do know it took the people of the city of Koln, Germany over 600 years to build their grandiose cathedral called the Dom. It houses some kings, relics, and bones. King Ludwig took a lot of the funds at the expense of the poor hardworking people to build it. I don't think we have 600 years. Besides, that would mean a lot more fundraisers. How about asking God for provision too? Let's not build something of our own will. Let's ask God what's important to His heart and what He sees for the future generations. Then let's come up with a better plan. He might tell us that we should sow a large sum into a need greater than our own. That's when we will see multiplication. Because you know we can't out give God. Our God is the God of impossibilities. He turns water into wine, multiplies fish and bread, brings sight to the blind, raises the dead, and parts the water. His greatness, goodness, and power never leaves us. So then, what building are we building in the kingdom now?

If you're like Mary, you ask Jesus for new wine, your cisterns will overflow with the best. Life in the Spirit looks above the mountain. If God wants us to heal the sick, raise the dead, fundraise, give that last widow's mite, or sing and dance like David danced, we will *go*! That's what building the kingdom should look like, at least to a charismatic or spirit-filled believer, revivalist or reformer. There are those who are called to the office of administration. God bless you all—we need the Martha's too. Oh, please Lord, let me be Mary! I love being in the secret place with you. I'd much rather pray for the gold coin to come forth from the fish's mouth and for the dead to be raised. I appreciate new strategies too, Lord. Please expand my thinking and horizon. Thank you, Lord. Horizon expanding! The *joy* of serving *you* by serving others is my journey as well. I'm caring in every way I possibly can for my eighty-nine-year-old dad and my grandchildren. I'm preparing a meal to share with family or friends, and other random acts of kindness.

This is all part of living a virtuous life. Seeking the Holy Spirit in all things leads us into building relationships and building God's Kingdom.

"In all things, seek ye first the Kingdom of God and his righteousness; and all these things shall be added unto you." – Matthew 6:33

"I will give you the keys of the Kingdom of heaven." – Matthew 16:19

I hear the whispers of the Lord saying, "Celebrate! Yes, celebrate again! Victory is yours, my beloved. I am has given my bride the Kingdom keys. Kingdom keys bring victory. Speak to the kingdom of opposition and darkness and release the Kingdom of light decrees. The decrees and declarations of Victory! Victory! Victory!

God's whispers resonate within my soul. I hear Him say, "Today 'I Am' is with you as I have always been. I am opening a new door for you that no man, demon, or principality can close. It is the key of authority in the greater works I have created for you. The plans and purposes I have for your life are so much more than you could ever imagine. Is there anything too big for your God? You, beloved, are mine. In my kingdom, there is no end. As you operate with your kingdom keys, mountains will come down. Let my light shine the way. Let my glory be your mantle. Let victory be your vision." Who will direct the plans?

CHAPTER EIGHT

Partnering With The Holy Spirit

"The Helper, the Holy Spirit, whom the Father will
send in my name, will teach you everything and
help you to remember all that I have told you."
–John 14:26

Whispers penetrating deeper and deeper into my soul as I hear the voice of my first love say, "You are my Pentecost girl! Smile! Come up higher, higher, higher, higher, higher, higher. I put the honey on your lips. I put the fire in your belly. I am your fire that burns. It is a perpetual fire in my kingdom and the kingdom is within you! Take the keys! Boldly take the keys! You have been given unmerited favor, extreme grace, wisdom, knowledge, and great love. My presence will never leave you or forsake you. Unmerited favor is yours, for you, beloved, are mine!"

In the fall of 2014, I attended an Aglow International Conference called "Carry His Presence," held in Albuquerque, New Mexico. It was a last-minute decision to attend as I pressed in with prayer that provision would be met. The distance and cost called for deeper pockets as well. I prayed fervently and provision was supplied. Yes, God does supply all our needs and gives us the desires of our heart too! I felt a strong tugging on my heart that the "Carry His Presence" conference released a fresh dimension of Father God's heart for His sons and daughters. Indeed, it was a strategic gathering of warriors and champions in God's Kingdom.

The following is an excerpt from the closing session of the "Carry His Presence" conference. It was a prophetic word given to Aglow International by one of our advisors, Graham Cooke. It is not by accident that the Holy Spirit led me to this prophetic release at this divine time for this chapter on partnering with the Holy Spirit. This, beloved of Christ, is who we are.

PROPHETIC WORD

We are aglow! We are passionate about Jesus. We are strong, vibrant, committed, a people without fear. We're making war on all negativity with joy. This peace is too strong for us to be anxious, worried, or panicked. Our mindset is rooted in majesty and we are rising to a new level of power. We are warriors. We know how to engage with God before we engage with the enemy. We know how to stand firm, to enter into presence. We are ordinary people transformed to become those who are strong and do exploits.

There is joy in intimate alignment that removes all the weariness of life. There's a place set aside for you where all struggle ceases and you enter into the fullness of rest and peace. And the Lord says, "as you worship me, as you wait on me in delight, you will be wonderfully renewed. It is intimate strength that I have arranged for you to view life from a higher realm. And as my spirit gives your spirit wings, so you will be raised up in your intimacy to be close to me. And you may come before the throne of grace and receive everything you need. You are my people, my beloved. And it is my absolute intention to raise you out of circumstances, out of a culture you no longer have any business being in, because I have redeemed you from that. And it is not your place to walk in those things. It is your place to walk in the high places with me. It is your place to sit with me far, far above, far above, far, far, far above and enjoy the view. I will supply you with the confidence so large it shall become a new boldness of Spirit. And you will have power to stand, to run, to walk without tiring. You will see miracles in your physical body, miracles in your physiology, that as you come into a place of intimacy; intimacy will act on you physically. And you will become stronger, more fit, more powerful, and you will not be debilitated in any way. You will have a new pick you up physically and will strengthen you powerfully. In your intimacy receive a fresh anointing to learn the power of rest and peace. Your soul is always untroubled when it lives in the shadow of your Spirit in Christ. I love rest," says the Lord. "And I love you. I will let you know my peace, which will always guard your heart and your mind. Everything I do is easy for me. I have no heavy burdens. My joy is so powerful, it lifts everything around me. This is what I have invited you into. This is your place, right here with me. I've given you a helper. Listen to him, allow no other voice to overshadow his, and we will commune with you. You're in Christ now. You are not your own. You have a different body. You're in Christ. That was our plan from the beginning to have you become one with us so that you would become like us, and we would live in you. Beloved, it's still the plan. It's time to extricate yourself from the affairs of this world, and become a citizen of heaven. And become involved in that dimension of life that we bring to you freely and joyfully. We're making you like us, and we love what we are doing in you and with you, and we love partnering with you. We love talking to you. We love listening to you. We love being with you. We love helping you. We love anointing you. We love lifting you up. We love encouraging you. We love working with you; stop working with the enemy. Work with us. We have better benefits. We have better benefits. We have no sickness package, though. You're in the Kingdom now; you're in the domain of the King. Learn how to abide there. Learn how to take advantage of everything that your God wants to give you. This is your day. This is your time to rise up and be absolutely, thoroughly brilliant."

Let's do it!

All in!

"The wind blows wherever it pleases. You hear its sound, but you cannot tell where it comes from or where it is going. So it is with everyone born of the Spirit." –John 3:8

Whispers of God telling me, "Listen, do you hear the sound of the rushing wind coming into the atmosphere? It is a whirlwind of shifting. It is a wind of change. Delight in me, my beloved, during these times of shifting, shaking, awakening, and releasing. For you are part of the Pentecost army. You are overshadowed by my presence, my goodness, and my mercy shall follow you all the days of your life."

"He that believeth on me, as the scripture says out
of his belly flow rivers of living water." –John 7:38

Got water?

CHAPTER NINE

Living Water

Whispers speaking words of wisdom, tell me to *trust.* "Trust in the provision that I have for you. Trust that I will see you through. Trust in my divine providence for you. Day to day, as you walk by faith in the Spirit, I am will continue to flourish you with the abundant inheritance that I have for you. You've prayed for restoration in families, ministries, cities and nations. I am the restorer of all. My purpose for you and for all remains the same. Stay in my peace and love. You have been planted in my abiding presence. Be joyful in hope of things yet to come. You are mine."

Whispers… "There are many who come to drink of my water then go about their everyday life with broken cisterns. They cannot sustain carrying the living water that never runs dry. The wells of their own making depletes their cisterns. Sustainability can only be accomplished through being connected to the source. By walking in forgiveness, repentance, and love keeps the water unpolluted and fresh. It is free of stagnation and breaches. I am has given you the keys. The kingdom of heaven is within you to protect and sanctify the well that you have been given. Keep holy what is holy. Walk in righteousness and love. For I have overcome the world and so will you. You are mine. I am your inheritance."

I hear the whispers of the Lord say, "Listen my beloved. Hear my voice calling unto you, come, come all who are weary and heavy-laden and I will give you rest. I am the Prince of Peace, and my presence operating in your life cultivates my peace and rest in you. Walk bravely in my peace throughout your life's journey home. Even in storms, my peace continues to calm the seas of tribulation. Let your heart and mind be full of my majesty that is the abundant life that carries you above the storm. It is my peace given for you."

"Peace I leave with you, my peace I give to you, not as
the world gives do I give to you. Let not your heart
be troubled, neither let it be afraid." -John 14:27

Oh Jesus, you are the living water that floods my soul! The years quickly pass and I ponder upon how vast and how great is our God. He placed a river of life within me. It is living within me! How could I not fathom and not grasp the treasure that you have given me? Overflowing river of love, joy, peace, goodness, grace, mercy, kindness, and so much more is living in me. I get to allocate a fresh drink with every breath I take. I can then pour it out in generous measure to those whom you have placed in my life.

There was a time, not long ago, that I felt so clueless about the immensity of that truth come alive within me. Needless to say, there was a river, but it didn't flow. It felt like a long drought and the water level was low.

It caused me to react to situations, people, challenges, and trials with complaining, self-pity, blame, bitterness, hopelessness, defeat, and anger. When things didn't go as smoothly as it should, I'd kick a hole in the wall or break something. Poor responses never create great outcomes. It's like eating ice-cream every night, not being mindful of fats and sugars that might lead to heart disease and a much larger wardrobe that is not measured in quantity, but in size. Perhaps likened to cussing the police officer for giving you a speeding ticket. How about going into battle without your boots on or without a battle plan? Where is true wisdom when wisdom isn't activated or pursued?

Think about how the Samaritan lady at the well comprehended that one. It was a good idea for her to imagine not ever having to be inconvenienced by having to draw water from the well again and haul it back home. Jesus prophetically revealed Himself then by saying the living water would be released from Him alone. He would be a spring of water welling up unto eternal life in us.

We have been given living water. How is that working for us? What is it producing?

Whispers in the morning, as I hear the Lord say, "Trials are passages into new beginnings. Especially through trials, let your hope be anchored in your Lord of Hosts. I carry you through every storm. Look to me and not your circumstances. Breakthrough is right around the corner. Be hopeful."

Are you still thirsty? What would a life with living water look like anyway? Come on, let's drink. The water level is rising.

CHAPTER TEN

Life In The Spirit

"But I say, walk by the Spirit, and you will not carry out the desire of the flesh. For the flesh sets its desire against the Spirit, and the Spirit against the flesh; for these are in opposition to one another, so that you may not do the things that you please."
– Galatians 5:16-17

"For you were formerly darkness, but now you are light in the Lord; walk as children of light."
– Ephesians 5:8

"Have you ever wondered what the atmosphere of heaven is like? Since God fills heaven with His light and glory, the atmosphere is all that God Himself is light, glory, goodness, joy, majesty…" – Excerpt from *Living Heaven to Earth and Loving It!* by Aglow International Leader President Jane Hansen-Hoyt

Whispers of my soul sing over me, the Lord is my eternal light and he has filled me with his Spirit! "Come away with me and I will give you rest. Come away with me and dine with me. I sing over you with joy and gladness. Be lifted up my beloved! Be lifted up for you are mine eternally!"

My heart responds, "Father, you are mine. You give me hope when I feel so hopeless. You give me strength when I am weak. You protect me in the midst of every storm. You shelter me from the tempest that rages fiercely against me. You guide me in your ways. You cover me with your robes of holiness and righteousness. Your love is everlasting. You are my eternal light! It is perpetual forever and ever, amen. Thank you, oh Lord. My love for you is eternal."

What's happening with my outrageous life in the spirit? What's happening with yours?

Have you ever felt your wick needed trimming because it could no longer burn and hold the flame? Jesus illustrated this well in the parable of the ten virgins who are also referred to as the wise and foolish virgins. The Gospel of Matthew 25:1-13 brings it to light when Jesus spoke and said, "That the five virgins who are prepared for the bridegroom's arrival are rewarded, while the five who are not prepared are disowned." Are we prepared? Is there enough oil within your abode to burn aflame? The one word that makes me shudder is *disowned!* Would you not tremble at the thought of being disowned by God? I would!

> "But whoever disowns me before others, I will disown
> before my Father in heaven." – Matthew 10:33

Jesus came that we would have life, and have it in the full. It's in our building blueprint the Bible. You can read it in John 10:10. However, a thief came too, and beloved, it wasn't to give you life. He came to steal, kill, and destroy. He is a devouring locust and the enemy of life. I implore you, choose life.

During the process of the third drafting of this book, I was awakened in the night and prompted by the Lord to write four things that would hinder our life in the Spirit:

1. Denying the dunamis power of God that is still alive and well in Spirit-filled believers.

2. Un-repented sin.

3. Worldly distractions.

4. Disunity and division in the body of Christ. Allowing bitter roots and un-forgiveness to rule.

I declare the rising up of warriors and champions for God's Kingdom. Sons and daughters of King Jesus who know who they are in Christ and the hunger and thirst for more of God's glory and majesty to be seen and known throughout the whole world.

Whispers in my soul, I here the Father say, "Rise up, keeper of the light and release it in power and might."

"For the Kingdom of God is not based on talk only
but on power." – 1 Corinthians 4:20

Awakened in the night hour I anxiously wait upon the Lord, knowing His manifest presence overshadows me as I hunger and I thirst for more of my beloved. Whispers say, "Come to my banquet table, my beloved. Come up higher and dine with me. Receive the new wine and fresh manna. Receive all that I am for you! I hold you so close to my heart. Can you feel my manifest presence? So often you are misunderstood. So often you have felt saddened and alone. Then you are enlightened and aware you are never alone. For the one whom your heart pants for has never left you. In that moment, your weakness is strengthened and your sadness turns to joy! For you, place your hope in me and you will never lack for anything. For you, my beloved, are mine and I am yours. Stay awhile, my sweet one. Come, come and dine with me. Won't you stay awhile?"

"My beloved is like a gazelle or a young stag; look, there he stands behind the wall, gazing through the windows, peering through the lattice. My beloved spoke and said to me, 'Arise, my darling, my beautiful one, come with me.'" – Song of Songs 2:9-12

Ready to roll warriors, champions and kingdom dragon slayers? Life in the Spirit means we are on the winning side. The battle of death was won at the cross by the perfect lamb, Jesus, who takes away the sin of the world. We have been given resurrection power to overcome the plans, schemes, wickedness, and evil intentions of the devil. We were made to conquer on earth as it is in heaven. God's good intention supersedes the evil deeds of the enemy's camp!

"For everyone who does evil hates the light, and does not come to the light for fear that his deeds will be exposed." – John 3:20

The clashes of the two kingdoms rage as the battles have been waged against the sons and daughters of the Kingdom of God.

"For we wrestle not against flesh and blood, but against principalities, against powers, against the rulers of the darkness of this world, against spiritual wickedness in high places." – Ephesians 6:12

How ready are we to take our rightful position in God's army? Are you battle ready? Because the battle has been won does not mean there won't be any more battles. Look around—battles are raging. What are your battles? Got upgraded armor?

CHAPTER ELEVEN

Armored For Battle

"When the enemy comes in like a flood, he shall raise a standard against him…" – Isaiah 59:19

Whispers of warning on April 20, 2012: "Beware of things to come. There are many who will waver from the truth. There are many that are blinded. They do not have ears to hear or eyes to see in the spirit realm. Their eyes and ears are focused upon worldly gains, worldly achievements, worldly status, worldly pleasures, and worldly accomplishments. Beware: there are many walking in darkness and like the father of lies, they rob, steal, and destroy. Yes, be wise and prudent. Release truth and hope for the captives, but remember always that we co-labor together. Do not run ahead of me. I am preparing the fallow ground for my warriors to penetrate and infiltrate to be victorious in my name, power, strength, and might. Beware of any other path to victory. I am delights in you. Walk bravely upon this journey. I am your mantle. I am your all in all. There is no fear in me. Walk bravely in my love, my compassion, my mercy, and my goodness. For your light has come. See and hear the sound of your deliverer, your King of Kings, your All in All!"

In a night vision, I am dressed in a new shiny armor. A beautiful, angelic being who had a feminine appearance entered the room. I had never been there before. There appeared demon entities crawling in multitudes on the walls. I sensed impending threats. It was frightening and intimidating. However, when the angelic being entered, I was both empowered and encouraged to stand my ground. The shiny new armor equipped me for battle. It was impenetrable from danger. Whispers in the night hour prepare the way.

The night visions continue to the next night of April 21, 2012. I am intently watching above as I see two large angels warring. They battled against each other with such force and thundering that it frightened me as I observed it. I looked up in this vision because it occured above me, in the second realm. While this is happening, I am confronted by a large in stature, Middle Eastern giant of a man. I was so scared, I tried to hide. However, I felt the courage of the Lord rise up in me as I looked up and confronted the giant. I declared Jesus is the way, the truth, and the life and there is only one true God.

There would be many more visions in the night hour as I kept watch. There are times in our journey that we will sense an urgency of Spirit to be a voice like John crying out in the desert that says, "Repent and be saved, for the Kingdom of God is at hand. We do not know the time or the hour and we must be ready."

I declare a mighty generation of warriors and champions are arising in God's Kingdom. They are the ones who have heard the battle cry. Their shields are in place and ready for battle. I declare walls are breaking, breaches are mended, and the truth is setting the captives free. Freedom in Christ!

THE PROPHETIC CLARION SOUND

Whispers decreeing the release of the clarion sound: "Sweet is the sound of my voice within you. Sweet is the sound. In days ahead, you will sing a clarion song. Your new song will touch others around you. For my voice will be a clarion shout out, resonating within you and pouring out of you. Be ready my daughter; laugh, sing, dance, and be full of joy, for your cup overfloweth!"

A clarion produces a sound that is clear. It is inspiring. It is a call to action and proclamation. It is time for that clarion sound to come forth. Releasing the sound of heaven!

Thank you Lord! Glory to you Oh Lord!

"Let love and faithfulness never leave you; bind them around your neck, write them on the tablet of your heart." – Proverbs 3:3

Whispers until the end: "Listen to what I have to say, and write this down. The time has come when all of mankind must choose to follow me or to continue to be a rebellious people and follow the ruler of this world, the ruler of darkness. Many are being deceived by the enticement and lies of the evil one. Many do not know their shepherd's voice. Let your roots go deep and be as a fruitful tree planted in my vineyard. I am coming soon."

Do you know the one calling out to you? The one who calls you His beloved? Profess it now. Let Him enter. Henceforth, profess it everyday: He is Lord who reigns and rules as King of Kings over your life. God continues to inhabit the praises of His people and delights to be the *Whispers in My Soul*. Enter into the secret place, beloved, and hear the whispers in your soul. May your Spirit man rise as you enter into new heights of life in the Spirit. Ascend, beloved, ascend! Hear the voice of the shepherd calling unto you, "Come up higher, for there is more!"

Our God reigns forever as King above all kings and His Kingdom will have no end.

> "Seek ye first the kingdom of God, and his righteousness; and all these things shall be added unto you."
> –Matthew 6:33

WHISPERS...

Establishing My Kingdom: "The kingdom of light is inhabited by my presence. The kingdom of light is void of sin, darkness, pain, or sorrow. It is established by my power and might. Be established in my kingdom. I give you the keys to lock or unlock. Be planted as mighty oaks as you get your nourishment from the presence of the Almighty, your King!"

Ephesians 2: Come alive in Christ. Read your blueprint.

CPSIA information can be obtained
at www.ICGtesting.com
Printed in the USA
FSOW03n1711101016
25985FS